7 contemporary piec

for BASSOON and P

UNBEATEN TRACKS

Edited by John Orford

CONTENTS

FABER ff MUSIC

PREFACE

I consider it a great compliment to be asked to contribute to the *Unbeaten Tracks* series. The bassoon is often over-looked as a solo instrument, and a fresh collection of not just interesting, but entertaining pieces is long overdue. I hope that the end result is as exciting for the young (or not so young!) bassoonist as it was for me to see the pieces come together.

This colourful and varied collection is a tribute to the composers' enthusiasm and skill. I hope that you enjoy playing these pieces, each with their different challenges, as much as I have. If one or two seem difficult at first, keep up the effort as the rewards are tremendous!

John Orford, March 2002

COMPOSER BIOPICS

All contributing composers were asked to give their own personal responses to the following questions; of course their answers can only reflect their views now and will be ever-changing:

Date and place of birth

Musical works that have most inspired you

Individuals who have most inspired you

What your piece means to you

A quote that you feel best describes your music in general

Your two favourite books

RICHARD BISSILL

Date and place of birth	14.02.60 Nottingham.
Inspiring musical works	*Symphonic Dances*, Sergey Rakhmaninov; Symphony No 5, Dmitry Shostakovich; *Sinfonietta*, Op 5, Erich Korngold; *La Valse*, Erich Korngold.
Inspiring individuals	John Bilton (music teacher), Garendon School, Loughborough; Philip Fowke (pianist); Robert Farnon (arranger/composer).
What your piece means to you	I composed this piece whilst staying on Orkney during the 2001 St Magnus Festival and it reminds me of the wonderful time I spent there.
A quote	Interesting, fun and challenging to play. Rich harmonies with slight jazz influences, strong melodies.
Two favourite books	*The Mayor of Casterbridge*, Thomas Hardy; *Perfume*, Patrick Süskind.

MICHAEL DAUGHERTY

Date and place of birth	28.04.54 Iowa, USA.
Inspiring musical works	Symphony No 4, Charles Ives; *Kind of Blue*, Miles Davis; Symphony No 9, Gustav Mahler; *Cold Sweat*, James Brown.
Inspiring individuals	My father, mother and four brothers (who are all musicians).
What your piece means to you	After composing *Bounce* for two bassoons, *Dead Elvis* for solo bassoon and chamber ensemble, and *Hell's Angels* for bassoon quartet and orchestra, it is exciting to compose a work that my thirteen-year-old daughter Evelyn can play on the bassoon.
A quote	My music is energetic, complex, fun, unusual, emotional, and inspired by American culture.
Two favourite books	*Goldfinger*, Ian Fleming; *2001: A Space Odyssey*, Arthur C Clarke.

CARL DAVIS

Date and place of birth	28.10.36 New York.
Inspiring musical works	*Mass in B minor*, Johann Sebastian Bach; *West Side Story*, Leonard Bernstein.
Inspiring individuals	Leonard Bernstein; Dietrich Fischer-Dieskau.
What your piece means to you	Beatrix Potter's Jeremy Fisher is a gentleman — and a frog. A bassoon is ideal for portraying both characters: it can be both poised, and can jump.
A quote	'… his music has a power that has you clutching the arms of your seat lest you be blown away.' (*The Observer*)
Two favourite books	*Middlemarch*, George Eliot; *The Catcher in the Rye*, J D Salinger.

JOSEPH PHIBBS

Date and place of birth	25.04.74 London.
Inspiring musical works	Symphony No 9, Gustav Mahler; *Petrushka*, Igor Stravinsky; *Partita*, Elliott Carter; *Pulse Shadows*, Harrison Birtwistle.
Inspiring individuals	Elliott Carter; Benjamin Britten.
What your piece means to you	I wanted to explore abrupt changes of mood; the lively outer sections of the piece are contrasted against an unusually dark and decadent-sounding tango. A stilted Latin flavour pervades through the piece.
A quote	I'm interested in exploring music in which different structures are evolving simultaneously. Melodic line is also important to me, as is harmony.
Two favourite books	*Four Quartets*, T S Eliot; *The Master and Margarita*, Mikhail Bulgakov.

BERND FRANKE

Date and place of birth	14.01.53 Weissenfels, Germany.
Inspiring musical works	*Sgt. Pepper's Lonely Hearts Club Band*, The Beatles; Symphony No 41, 'Jupiter', Wolfgang Amadeus Mozart; *The Unanswered Question*, Charles Ives; *The Art of Fugue*, Johann Sebastian Bach; celtic music; jazz; world music.
Inspiring individuals	Louis Kresner (who premiered the violin concertos by Anton Webern and Arnold Schoenberg), and Leonard Bernstein — both of whom I met in 1989 in Tanglewood, USA. Also Jean Guitton (French philosopher).
What your piece means to you	An incredible experience from a journey in 1999 to Bali and Java. 'Prambanan' is the most impressive Hindu temple in Java and has been a great event in my life — very spiritual!
A quote	'Bernd Franke's work distinguishes itself from other types of music […] not only by its elegance and hedonistic character, but ultimately by the way such contrasts are minutely built up and stressed through an ever-sharpening differentiation of sounds.' (Gisela Nauck, Berlin)
Two favourite books	*Dieu et la science*, Jean Guitton; *L'Identité*, Milan Kundera

FRASER TRAINER

Date and place of birth	14.05.67 Chelmsford, Essex.
Inspiring musical works	*Mass in B minor*, Johann Sebastian Bach; *One Nation under a Groove*, Funkadelic; anything by Igor Stravinsky.
Inspiring individuals	Mark-Anthony Turnage (composer); Eugene Skeef (South African percussionist).
What your piece means to you	It's a song for a character in a short story called *The Colour of Scars* by Florri McMillan. The opening and closing bassoon theme is derived from material in my saxophone concerto which is based on the same story.
A quote	'Sheer good old-fashioned inspiration.'
Two favourite books	*Longitude*, Dava Sobel; *The Good Food Guide 2002*.

PAUL HART

Date and place of birth	16.03.54 Ilford, Essex.
Inspiring musical works	The symphonies of Ludwig van Beethoven; *Mother Goose Suite*, Maurice Ravel; *The Rite of Spring*, Igor Stravinsky; Double violin concerto in D, Johann Sebastian Bach.
Inspiring individuals	My first violin teacher, A W Young; my piano teacher, A Hill; my first composition teacher, J Baird; the saxophonist and composer, John Dankworth.
What your piece means to you	*Andante* is a lyrical piece that you should use to try and charm your audience.
A quote	Sometimes quirky, sometimes sentimental, normally written with an audience in mind, and, hopefully, always well-crafted.
Two favourite books	*Our Man in Havana*, Graham Greene; *Fairytale of New York*, J P Donleavy.

© 2002 by Faber Music Ltd
First published in 2002 by Faber Music Ltd
3 Queen Square London WC1N 3AU
Cover by Økvik Design
Music processed by Wessex Music Services
Printed in England by Caligraving Ltd

ISBN 0-571-52004-9

To buy Faber Music publications or to find out about the full range of titles available please contact your local music retailer or Faber Music sales enquiries:

Faber Music Ltd, Burnt Mill, Elizabeth Way, Harlow CM20 2HX
Tel: +44 (0)1279 82 89 82   Fax: +44 (0)1279 82 89 83
sales@fabermusic.com   www.fabermusic.com

Tango rouge

Joseph Phibbs

Meno mosso (♩ = c.50)
molto rubato e espressivo (à la tango)

Mr Jeremy Fisher

Carl Davis

to my thirteen-year-old daughter Evelyn, who plays a mean bassoon

Bell-bottom blues

Michael Daugherty

14

* white-note gliss.

Hector unravelled

Richard Bissill

7 contemporary pieces
for BASSOON and PIANO

UNBEATEN TRACKS

Edited by John Orford

BASSOON PART

CONTENTS

© 2002 by Faber Music Ltd
First published in 2002 by Faber Music Ltd
3 Queen Square London WC1N 3AU
Cover by Økvik Design
Music processed by Wessex Music Services
Printed in England by Caligraving Ltd
All rights reserved

ISBN 0-571-52004-9

To buy Faber Music publications or to find out about the
full range of titles available please contact your local music
retailer or Faber Music sales enquiries:
Faber Music Ltd, Burnt Mill, Elizabeth Way, Harlow CM20 2HX
Tel: +44 (0)1279 82 89 82   Fax: +44 (0)1279 82 89 83
sales@fabermusic.com   www.fabermusic.com

Tango rouge

Joseph Phibbs

Mr Jeremy Fisher

Carl Davis

to my thirteen-year-old daughter Evelyn, who plays a mean bassoon

Bell-bottom blues

Michael Daugherty

Hector unravelled

Richard Bissill

Song for Connie

Fraser Trainer

8

Prambanan*

Bernd Franke

* For legend and suggested fingerings, see page 12.

Andante

Paul Hart

Prambanan

Legend

‡	Quarter tone higher
♯♯	Three-quarter tone higher

Suggested fingerings

Bars 6, 7, 11	A ‡ (+A♭ key)
Bars 6,7	E ‡ (+A♭ key)
Bar 11	A ♯♯ (+F key)
Bar 11	B ‡ (+B♭ key)
Bar 12	G ‡ (+B♭ key)
Bar 12	G ♯♯ (Play A +RH1 +F♯ key)
Bar 12	A ‡ (+A♭ key)
Bar 12	B ‡ (-LH1)

accel. poco a poco al fine

Song for Connie

Fraser Trainer

Prambanan

Bernd Franke

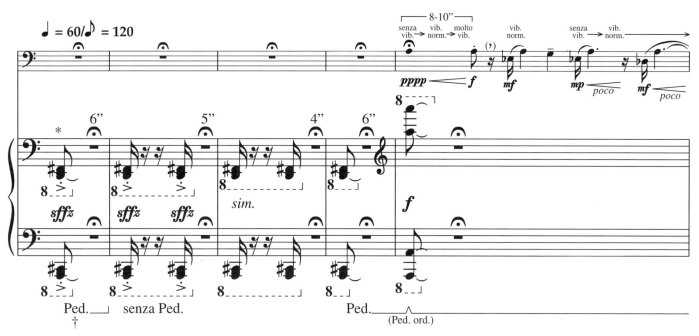

* five-note (chromatic) cluster
† Ped. after chord, but catch the sound before the hands release

28

Andante

Paul Hart